# Taking Control of Your Money

# Taking Control of Your Money

**A Financial Guide for Young Professionals**

*Second Edition*

**J. P. KILASARA**

BELLS PUBLISHERS

Published by Bells Publishers a division of Bells Business Solutions, LLC.
www.bellsbusiness.com

Printed in the United States of America

ISBN-13: 978-0-6152-9021-8

ISBN-10: 0-6152-9021-3

# Contents

Introduction ........................................................................................... ix

STEP 1:  Review current personal financial status ............................................. 1

STEP 2: Create a personal budget ................................................................. 5

STEP 3: Establish financial goals ................................................................. 11

STEP 4: Develop strategies to fund financial goals .......................................... 17

STEP 5: Investment Planning ..................................................................... 23

STEP 6: Insurance Planning ....................................................................... 37

STEP 7: Retirement Planning ..................................................................... 43

STEP 8: Saving for kids' education .............................................................. 55

STEP 9: Starting a business ....................................................................... 59

STEP 10:  Teaching children about money .................................................... 81

Resources ............................................................................................. 89

## In memory of

Aunt Uyanjo (1960 – 1991)


You helped me turn my hobby into a business.

Thank you Mama Mdogo!

# Introduction

Financial planning is an important but challenging process. In this book, the author will provide a step-by-step guide for young professionals on how to take control of their money through financial planning.

The author discusses simple ways of increasing personal income and reducing personal expenditure in order to **Increase Savings**, **Start Investing** and **Manage Money**.

There are two main parts to the equation of savings, that is:

*Income - Expenditure = Savings*

There are 2 main ways to Increase Savings: Increase Income or Reduce Expenditure.

**Personal financial planning** is a process whereby an individual (on their own or with the help of a financial advisor) does an assessment of his/her present financial status, develops their financial goals and objectives, and creates a plan to achieve those goals.

**A personal financial plan** is basically a plan of how future income is allocated towards achieving personal financial goals.

It involves setting up an emergency fund, planning for family expenses, investment planning (to generate more income through savings), retirement planning (to maintain current standard of living), insurance planning (to protect investments for the benefit of dependants should anything happen to you) and saving for children's education.

***For example:*** A long-term financial goal could be, "I would like to retire at age 55 with a personal net worth of US$ 80,000 or Tshs. 80 million in order to maintain my current standard of living."

The planning and accomplishment of such a goal would depend on a number of other factors such as life expectancy, monthly income needs at retirement, current income and current expenditure, expected interest rate, expected inflation rate and other expected income during retirement such as from pension or relatives.

Happy Financial Planning!

## Special thanks

To Dad, Mr. Philip Puja and Mom, Dr. Grace Puja,
Thank you for everything you have taught us.
God bless you always!

# STEP 1: Review current personal financial status

| In summary, this chapter will cover: |
| :--- |
| - The difference between assets and liabilities |
| - Calculation of personal net worth |
| - The personal Net Worth worksheet |

The first step in the financial planning process is to determine the current financial position by calculating personal net worth. Personal net worth is important when applying for a loan.

**Personal Net worth** is the difference between personal assets and personal liabilities.

Simply put, an asset is what belongs to you and a liability is that which is owed to others.

**Assets** include but are not limited to:

- Cash

- Bank account balances

- Market value of house

- Market value of car

- Company shares

- Bonds

- Pension

- Home furnishings (such as paintings, furniture, computer, electronics and other equipment)

- Jewelry

- Cash value of life insurance

- Value of personal business, etc

**Liabilities** include but are not limited to:

- Long-term loans such as student loan, mortgage/home loan

- Short-term loans such as car loan, personal bank loan, credit card loan and money owed to individuals

- Outstanding taxes

- Other financial obligations such as law suits, etc

***Tip:*** The secret to increasing one's net worth is to preserve one's earnings by increasing investments/assets and reducing liabilities.

## Net Worth Worksheet

| ASSETS | Amount | LIABILITIES | Amount |
|---|---|---|---|
| | | | |
| **Cash and cash equivalents** | | Home loan | |
| Cash | | Bank/personal loan | |
| Bank savings account | | Student loan | |
| SACCO savings account | | Car loan | |
| Fixed Deposit | | Credit card loan | |
| **Shares and bonds** | | Store card loan | |
| Shares | | Insurance payments | |
| Bonds | | Income taxes | |
| Mutual funds | | Property taxes | |
| Unit Trust | | Other taxes | |
| Other | | Other debt | |
| **Real Estate** | | | |
| Market value of house | | | |
| Market value of vacation house | | | |
| Rental house | | | |
| Other | | | |
| **Retirement assets** | | | |
| Pension | | | |
| Savings plan | | | |
| Other | | | |
| **Personal Property** | | | |
| Vehicles | | | |
| Jewelry | | | |
| Other | | | |
| **Insurance** | | | |
| Cash value of life insurance | | | |
| Other | | | |
| **Other investments** | | | |
| Ownership in businesses | | | |
| Home furniture, electronics etc | | | |
| Other | | | |
| **Total Assets** | | **Total Liabilities** | |
| **Net Worth (Assets minus Liabilities) =** | | | |

# STEP 2: Create a personal budget

| In summary, this chapter will cover: |
| --- |
| - Benefits of using a personal budget |
| - How to effectively maintain a budget |
| - The budget worksheet |

The next step after calculating personal net worth is to create a monthly budget to monitor income and expenditures. This will help determine how much income is available every month for fulfilling short-term and long-term financial goals.

**A personal budget** comprises of total expenses and total income of a person or household for a specified time period such as a month.

If large corporations operate on budgets, it shows how important budgets are regardless of how much an individual earns. The main difference is how each individual maintains their budget.

People manage personal budgets in different ways. This chapter will elaborate a simplified but detailed way of maintaining a budget. These steps can be customized to suit personal needs.

## Some of the benefits of creating a budget

- A budget is one of the initial important steps towards effective financial planning
- It gives a bigger picture of where most of the money is being spent in relation to income and enables adjustments to be done where necessary

- Helps establish and maintain healthy spending habits
- Makes decision making much easier when choosing where to spend money and where not to
- It helps an individual or household stay organized if the budget is maintained in a consistent manner

## A simple but detailed way to create a budget

- Keep receipts in labeled envelopes and write down all expenses and bills on paper, spreadsheet or another software

- At the end of each month for a period of at least 3 months, review and record prices for each item

- Use the list to prepare an annual budget, some items might be purchased each month while others might be purchased every other month or so

- On the budget create at least 4 columns; Description, budget amount, actual amount and percentage

- The description column will contain detailed explanation of the expense

- The budget amount is the amount expected to be spent on each item

- The actual amount is what has already been spent for each item

- The percentage column will show what portion of income each item takes away

- Create a budget for each month taking into account items that are purchased once every two or more months

- To record more details and keep a more accurate account of items a weekly budget can also be created

# How to make the budget work

- Distinguish between needs and wants. A need is something you cannot do without while a want is something that can wait for funds availability

- For variable expenses such as telephone expenses decide how much is necessary and stick to it to ensure that only an amount within reasonable individual limits is spent

- Create a list of items to be purchased when shopping and list the prices to use as a guideline to avoid overspending

- When it comes to purchasing items that cost a lot and are not in the regular budget, it is important to do some research from multiple sellers and record prices to determine which one is the most affordable

- Keep a copy of the budget at a convenient place where it would be easily accessible on a daily basis

- Keep receipts and use them to record the actual amount for each item immediately after shopping

- Review the budget on a monthly basis and update if necessary

- Savings should be a part of the monthly bills. Setup direct deposit for savings if possible or use any other means to ensure that savings are set aside into a separate account before other bills are paid.

- Bargain to get the best prices when purchasing items whose prices can be reduced

- Take advantage of coupons or discounts whenever available to get the best price for each item bought

- Avoid purchasing brand name items whenever there are similar non-brand items that can fulfill the same need

- Pre-used items that are still in good condition can provide the same amount of satisfaction as new items but at a lower price

- Use labeled envelopes to set aside money to purchase items on a monthly basis to ensure that only the amount set aside is used

- If a vacation is planned start setting aside funds ahead of time (such as a year in advance) to avoid last minute pressure

- Start setting aside funds for emergency - the recommended amount is usually an amount equal to at least 3 months' income - this will help maintain the budget during emergencies

- If you have kids, teach them about money and involve them in the planning process based on their age. The last chapter in this book discusses how to teach kids about money

In the next section a monthly budget worksheet is provided for use as a template.

**INCOME** column reflects money received or earned during the month from various sources.

**EXPENSES** column is for all money used or spent during the month to pay for various items.

**BUDGET AMOUNT** column is for planning purposes. This column is used to write down how much money is to be spent on each of the monthly expenditures.

**ACTUAL AMOUNT** column is used to track down the actual amount spent on expenses to determine if the final expenditure exceeded the budgeted amount so that this can be corrected or monitored in the following month.

**PERCENTAGE COLUMN** gives an idea of which expenses are taking up a large portion of income.

Each item's percentage value can be obtained by taking the actual amount for the individual item and dividing it by the total amount at the bottom of the Actual column.

Strategies can be established so as to make adjustments if necessary in order to increase amount of savings every month.

***Tip:*** Focus on personal needs rather than wants or peer pressure.

## Monthly Budget Worksheet

| Income | Amount | Expenses | Budget | Actual | Percentage |
|--------|--------|----------|--------|--------|------------|
| | | | Amount | Amount | % |
| | | **Household expenses** | | | |
| Salary | | Rent/Mortgage payment | | | |
| Bonus | | Electricity & Water | | | |
| Business income | | Telephone & Cable TV | | | |
| Capital gains | | Food | | | |
| Dividends | | Children's expenses | | | |
| Interest income | | Transportation (daladala) | | | |
| Tips/gratuity | | Maintenance & Repairs | | | |
| Gifts | | Extended family assistance | | | |
| Rental income | | **Loan installments** | | | |
| Commission | | Other house loans | | | |
| Other | | Student & personal loans | | | |
| | | Other | | | |
| | | **Insurance premiums** | | | |
| | | Car insurance | | | |
| | | Life insurance | | | |
| | | Disability insurance | | | |
| | | Home insurance | | | |
| | | **Other expenses** | | | |
| | | Savings (at least 10%) | | | |
| | | School fees & expenses | | | |
| | | Medical expenses | | | |
| | | Personal Care | | | |
| | | Personal Care | | | |
| | | Entertainment & vacation | | | |
| | | Vehicle expenses | | | |
| | | Other-1 | | | |
| | | Other-2 | | | |
| | | Other-3 | | | |
| **Total Income** | | **Total Expenses** | | | |
| **Expected Surplus/Deficit (Income minus Expenses) =** | | | | | |
| **Actual Surplus/Deficit (Income minus Expenses) =** | | | | | |

# STEP 3: Establish financial goals

| In summary, this chapter will cover: |
| --- |
| - Establishment of financial goals |
| - How to manage personal debt |
| - The financial goals worksheet |

Once a budget has been created, it is important to start working on how to allocate future income towards investments that will help increase and strengthen your net worth. Establishing financial goals gives an idea of where you want to be, when and how to get there. Set up goals in categories of short, medium and long-term.

It is important to review all financial goals at least once every year. This will provide room for making updates that might be necessary and it also provides a chance to cross off any goals that have been accomplished. It gives some people great satisfaction to be able to cross off goals that have been attained.

Financial goals differ among people. Below are examples that can serve as a general guideline.

## Short-term financial goals (1 to 2 years) examples:

- Set up an emergency fund
- Plan for your wedding

- Attend a higher learning institution

- Start supporting a family member's education

- Buy furniture, computer or other electronics

## Medium-term financial goals (2 to 5 years) examples:

- Start a family

- Buy a plot and building a house or buying a house

- Purchase a car

- Start planning annual vacations

- Reduce personal debt

- Start saving for retirement

## Long-term financial goals (5 to 10 years) examples:

- Start a business

- Build a vacation home (second or third home etc)

- Start saving for children's education

After listing all financial goals, a strategic plan of how to accomplish these goals needs to be determined and implemented to ensure that the goals are reached.

Establishing financial goals helps us see the bigger picture of our future financial status. Having financial goals is crucial even when there is no income being generated in the present.

The next section shows a Financial Goals Worksheet that can be used to plan and organize financial goals.

## Financial Goals Worksheet

| SHORT-TERM GOALS | AMOUNT | STATUS |
|---|---|---|
| | | |
| eg.  Setup an emergency fund | Tshs. 5,000,000 | Completed |
| | | |
| | | |
| | | |
| | | |
| | | |
| **MEDIUM-TERM GOALS** | **AMOUNT** | **STATUS** |
| eg.  Buy a plot for building a house | Tshs. 10, 000,000 | In-process-50% done |
| | | |
| | | |
| | | |
| | | |
| | | |
| | | |
| **LONG-TERM GOALS** | **AMOUNT** | **STATUS** |
| eg.  Start saving for children's education | Tshs.  10,000,000 | Not yet started |
| | | |
| | | |
| | | |
| | | |
| | | |
| | | |

# How to manage personal debt

For some, borrowing may be something that is completely out of the question for a variety of reasons. However for some, borrowing may help meet important financial needs.

Borrowing can be worth it if the money is used to:

- Finance a business
- Buy or build a house
- Purchase a needed car as opposed to an extra car
- Buy other durable items

Borrowing is not recommended if the funds are used to finance consumable items especially if the entire amount of the debt cannot be paid within the same month; these items include:

- Buying clothing
- Purchasing jewelry
- Financing a vacation
- Buying other luxurious items

## Borrowing principles

- Spending should be closely monitored to ensure that the money goes where it was intended.
- When paying off the loan, priority should be placed on loans with the highest interest rate.

- If the loan is on credit card, be sure to pay a monthly payment that is above the minimum so as to reduce the overall cost (interest) in the long run.

- It is not advisable to take a loan whose monthly payments cannot be afforded because the risk of defaulting is high.

- If possible, consolidate all credit card debt into one card with the lowest rate, this may help ease up the financial burden of having to pay multiple cards every month and may reduce the interest amount paid.

For individuals with access to applying for credit cards such as store cards, resist the urge to apply for multiple cards; it is not worth the 10% or 15% discount applied to the first purchase because in the long run most people end up with a huge credit card debt with no way of paying it off.

Maintain only a few credit cards for purposes of creating a good credit history, which comes in handy when applying for a house or car loan.

## Credit History and borrowing

Some countries have a credit system that allows for companies to access information or records belonging to each individual using a specific identification number. One of the reasons is to obtain a record of an individual's credit history, which basically shows how trustworthy the individual is. Credit companies can access these records and determine whether the person is trustworthy enough to be given a certain amount of money as a loan. In countries such as the US, this system also assigns credit scores or numbers. Individuals can access these records to review their information by requesting copies of their credit report.

# How to create a good credit history

- Pay all debts on time to avoid being charged late fees because these affect the credit report.

- Avoid defaulting on any of the loans – that is, pay all debts until they are completely paid off and there are no outstanding balances.

- Resist applying for multiple credit cards this affects the application for a mortgage or car loan.

- Monitor credit history by obtaining copies of credit reports from all major credit bureaus for comparison. This ensures that the report is correct and that no activity is attributed to someone else's purchases as a result of identity theft or fraud. In the USA there are three credit bureaus namely Equifax, Experian and TransUnion.

- Some creditors or credit card companies automatically increase credit limits (the maximum amount they can let an individual borrow) and they may also automatically reduce interest rates after a certain time based on the person's repayment history. However, an individual can also call and ask for an increase on the credit limit or a lower interest rate. This is important when applying for a loan such as a house or car loan since a higher credit limit may indicate trustworthiness and a lower interest rate may show that others consider the individual to be less risky.

***Tip:*** Review and adjust financial goals every year in order to remain on target.

# STEP 4: Develop strategies to fund financial goals

| In summary, this chapter will cover: |
| --- |
| - The importance of setting up an emergency fund |
| - Management of an effective savings plan |
| - Personal notes worksheet |

After the exciting process of establishing financial goals we now focus on the more detailed aspect of developing strategies to set aside money/funds to meet the goals established in step 3.

The following factors need to be considered when developing a strategy:

- Open accounts into which each goal's funds will be kept and allowed to grow

- Develop a savings plan that will facilitate the accomplishment of goals

- How much money will be needed to fund each financial goal?

- How much time is needed to accomplish the established goals?

- How much money needs to be set aside each month to meet these goals?

# Setting up an Emergency Fund

- It is recommended to set aside money equivalent to at least 3 to 6 months of the household gross income. This money is to be used in case of an emergency, such as loss of employment or for unexpected medical expenses etc.

- It is important to replenish the fund by returning any money taken out as soon as the next salary/income is received to avoid depleting the emergency fund.

- To establish an emergency fund choose a type of account that is highly conservative (less risky) and highly liquid (an account that can easily be converted into cash). This will facilitate access when there is a financial emergency. A good example is a Savings account and for those with large sums of money a Money Market account will serve the purpose where available since they tend to offer higher interest rates compared to regular savings accounts.

# How to start and manage an effective savings plan

- **Pay yourself.** Set aside 10% of income in a savings account. It is advised that this amount be set aside every month before other expenses are paid for. Starting a savings plan with any amount is better than having none at all. This money can later be invested after thorough research has been done to find out the viability of the investment options. For those who tithe, there is 10% of income to be given out before taking care of any other expenses including the 10% personal savings amount.

- **Emergency Fund.** Set aside money worth at least 3 – 6 months of the monthly gross salary into an emergency fund. This is recommended for any savings plan as has been discussed in the previous section.

- **Create a budget.** Creating a budget and sticking to it helps keep in line with priorities and helps avoid shopping surprises.

- **Discipline.** The key to managing a savings plan and making the budget work is to develop a specific routine on how to spend money with specific guidelines based on the budget. This can help maintain the discipline needed.

- **Making sacrifices.** Eliminating or reducing some expenses may help release some cash. Purchases of expensive jewelry, clothes, shoes and expensive gadgets can be reduced and kept to a minimum. For example, try taking homemade food to work instead of buying lunch every day. Eating home cooked meals rather than eating out or buying take-out helps reduce the expense side of the budget.

- **Identify necessities.** Avoid budgeting for and purchasing items that you can do without. For example, sodas can be substituted with regular purified tap water as a healthy and less expensive alternative.

- **List items for shopping.** Create a list of items that need to be purchased and try as much as possible to follow it. Establish a regular shopping routine to minimize unplanned and expensive shopping sprees.

- **Bargain**. One of the key tips to successful bargaining is to state your original price lower than what you are able to pay so that when you finally reach a deal, it will be within your price range.

- **Avoid peer pressure.** This can be accomplished by focusing on personal financial goals to eliminate unexpected expenditures.

Having financial goals helps give a bigger picture of the future and therefore eliminates the need to buy everything that others are buying which is likely to go against your financial goals.

- **Salary increase.** This could boost up savings if the additional income received is put away immediately into a separate savings account. In order to enjoy a salary raise, use it to fund a financial goal that was still pending by saving the amount of the salary increase on a monthly basis.

- **Additional income.** Generation of extra income through hobbies and other business projects can add up a significant amount of income. Take time to research available and affordable options.

- **Saving coins and smaller notes.** Try spending notes or bills alone and save all coins in a special piggy bank. This could also be a regular container with a tight lid. Afterwards, the accumulated money can be taken to the bank to be deposited or it can be invested so that it can continue to accumulate.

- **Plan ahead**. Planning to save for specific financial goals ahead of time will help minimize significant shifts in the savings pattern when there is a major purchase that needs to be done. This will reduce the need for a large sum of money to be drawn from the regular budget to finance the major purchase.

- **Multiple accounts.** Maintain multiple savings or fixed deposit accounts and match these accounts with specific financial goals to facilitate the accomplishment of these goals.

- **Helping relatives.** Giving to others is as important as spending it on your self. It is a blessing to help others in the immediate or extended family while supporting their efforts to become financially independent.

- **Give to charity**. The difference between giving and receiving is the fact that donations can bring a smile to another person's life. In addition to giving to family members and friends, gifts/donations can be given to officially established centers or institutions with specific projects.

- **Vacation.** After long hours at work everyone deserves a vacation. Planning and saving for vacations ahead of time may make it easier to enjoy the vacation somewhere away from home without major financial constraints. However, a vacation can still be possible when facing financial hardships if we can just be creative and find fun ways to spend the vacation or search online for simple fun activities to do at little or no cost at all.

- **Save it!** Collect all the income that was saved from all the steps above and put it into a savings account before it gets spent on other things. Once you manage to save some extra cash it is important to put that money into a designated account so as to meet the financial goals that you had planned for.

In summary, after reviewing the current financial status, generating a personal monthly budget and establishing financial goals, it is then possible to develop strategies on how to increase savings by finding ways to get more income and reduce expenses in order to focus on reaching the financial goals that were established.

***Tip:*** An emergency fund is the most important financial goal to start saving for, then other goals may follow.

The next section provides a template that can be used to write down personal strategies for accomplishing financial goals.

**Personal Notes Worksheet**

| Strategies on How to: | | |
|---|---|---|
| **Increase Income** | **Reduce Expenses** | **Reach financial goals** |
| eg. Start a photography business | eg. No more unnecessary electronic gadgets | eg. Open account for each major goal |
| eg. Get a part time job on weekends | eg. Take the bus instead of taxi | eg. Maintain a current list of all financial goals |
| | | |
| | | |
| | | |
| | | |
| | | |
| | | |
| | | |
| | | |
| | | |
| | | |
| | | |
| | | |
| | | |
| | | |

# STEP 5: Investment Planning

| In summary, this chapter will cover: |
| --- |
| - Categories of investment |
| - Investment options in Tanzania, Kenya and Uganda |
| - Review of a sample investment portfolio |
| - Management of risk while investing |
| - Importance of writing a Last Will |

Once strategies are in place, the next step is to research and choose the appropriate investment vehicles for implementing the strategies.

It is important to choose investments based on financial goals and based on when money will be needed to fund these goals.

According to the American Heritage Dictionary the definition of **Investing** is: To commit (money or capital) in order to gain a financial return.

The American Heritage Dictionary also defines **an Investment** as: A Property or another possession acquired for future financial return or benefit.

## Three major categories of investment vehicles

- Cash (such as bank savings accounts etc.)

- Stocks/shares including Mutual Funds

- Bonds; Government and Corporate

**Cash** refers to currency, bank savings accounts and other accounts that can be easily converted to cash (liquid assets). In some countries such as the US, money market accounts provide an additional option for highly liquid assets. They offer higher interest compared to regular savings accounts and require short or no notice for withdrawals, however may have additional restrictions.

**Stock/share** is a share of ownership in a company, which can be either common stock or preferred stock. Common stock usually carries voting rights in corporate decisions, while preferred stock does not have voting rights but is entitled to receive a certain amount of dividend payments before any dividends can be paid to other shareholders. However, not all equity shares are the same and it is important to understand the unique and specific clauses that affect each type of share bought.

**A bond** is a debt security issued by corporations and governments. It is a form of a loan to the corporation or government to help finance current operations and other acquisitions. The bond issuer is obliged to repay the bondholder the principal and interest at a specified later date (maturity date). A bondholder does not have ownership of the corporation or government; rather the bondholder is a lender.

**Examples of specific goals and their possible investment options**

- **Emergency fund:** Savings account
- **College funding for a 3 year-old child:** Company shares
- **College funding for a 17 year-old child:** Bonds maturing in 3 – 6 years and when school starts, Time Deposits with terms that are close to the start of the school year.

# Investment Portfolio sample

An Investment Portfolio is a mix of investments held by an individual or an entity. Below is an example of an investment portfolio that comprises all investment categories, that is Cash, Company shares and Bonds.

**Investment Portfolio for Maisha Mapambano – Age 25 years**

| Investment Type | Investment Value | Percentage |
|---|---|---|
| Savings account | 300,000 | 8% |
| Checking account | 100,000 | 3% |
| Time Deposit | 400,000 | 11% |
| Mutual Fund-Umoja Fund | 500,000 | 14% |
| Twiga company shares | 600,000 | 16% |
| TATEPA company shares | 800,000 | 22% |
| Treasury Bills | 1,000,000 | 27% |
| **Total Value of Portfolio** | **3,700,000** | **100%** |

Below is a pie chart illustration of Maisha Mapambano's portfolio

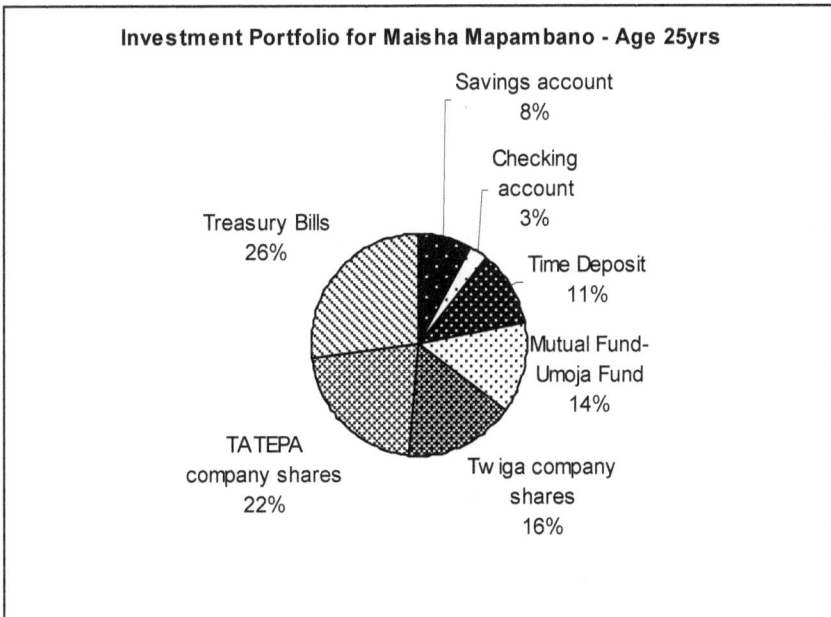

Investment Portfolio for Maisha Mapambano - Age 25yrs

# Available investment options in Tanzania

- Savings Accounts (Banks and Non-Banks such as SACCOs)
- Fixed Deposits
- Government Bonds – 10 bonds listed with the Dar es Salaam Stock Exchange (DSE)
- Corporate Bonds – 7 bonds listed with the DSE
- Company Shares/Stocks – 15 companies listed with the DSE
- Collective Investment Schemes – Umoja Fund and NICO (National Investment Company)
- Direct real estate for rental or for selling

### Company shares

In Tanzania company shares can be bought and sold at the Dar es Salaam Stock Exchange. Individual investors who are interested in buying and selling CRDB shares can do so over the counter at the bank branches.

# Commissions and other costs

### Bond Investors

A bond investor pays a 1.16% commission for transactions of Tshs. 40,000,000 and below. For additional amounts above Tshs. 40m, the investor pays 1.32% in commissions. The minimum commission is Tshs. 5,000.

### Equity Investors

For transactions worth Tshs. 10,000,000 (initial investment), an equity investor pays 1.70% in broker's commission, 0.28% in transaction fees, 0.02% in Fidelity fund fee. This means the total cost to the investor will be 2.00%.

On the next Tshs. 40ml, an investor incurs 1.5% in broker's commission, 0.28% in transaction fees, 0.02% in Fidelity fund fee, which brings the total cost to 1.80%.

Finally, for any amounts above Tshs. 50ml the investor pays 0.8% in broker's commission, 0.28% in transaction fee and 0.02% in fidelity fund fee. The total cost for these transactions will be 1.80%.

**Notes:**

- According to the Dar Stock Exchange website, Fidelity Fund is a fund established to compensate investors who suffer pecuniary loss from any defalcation committed by Licensed Dealing Member companies in relation to any money or property that has been entrusted to the DSE member company. This compensation however is only limited to Tshs. 100,000.

For commissions and other costs to the investor visit the DSE website at www.dse.co.tz

# Tax advantages of trading on DSE listed equities

There is a number of tax advantages of trading on the DSE listed equities compared to unlisted equities.

- The withholding tax on dividend payable is 5% on listed equities compared to 10% on unlisted equities.

- The stamp duty on transfer of security is not charged for listed equities compared to a 6% charge for unlisted equities.

- There is no capital gain tax on disposal (sale) of securities for listed equities, while 10% is imposed on unlisted equities.

# 15 listed companies whose shares can be bought at the DSE are:

- TOL Limited (TOL)

- Tanzania Breweries Limited (TBL)

- Tanzania Tea Packers Limited (TATEPA)

- Tanzania Cigarette Company Limited (TCC)

- Tanga Cement Company Limited (SIMBA)

- SWISSPORT Tanzania Limited (SWISSPORT)

- Tanzania Portland Cement Company Limited (TWIGA)

- Kenya Airways Limited (KA)

- East African Breweries Ltd (EABL)

- Jubilee Holdings Ltd (JHL)

- National Investment Company Limited

- Dar Es Salaam Community Bank

- National Microfinance Bank Plc

- Kenya Commercial Bank Limited

- CRDB Bank Public Limited Company

## Licensed dealing members/Brokers at the DSE are:

- Tanzania Securities Limited

- Rasilimali Limited

- Solomon Securities Limited

- Orbit Securities Co. Limited

- Vertex International Securities Limited

- Core Securities Ltd.

## Investment Advisors

- African Banking Corporation

- Aureos Tanzania Managers Limited

- Barclays Bank Tanzania Limited

- Consultants For Resources Evaluation Limited

- Deloitte Consulting Limited

- Orbit Securities Limited

- Rasilimali Limited

- Standard Chartered Bank (T) Limited

- Tanzania Securities Limited

- Unit Trust of Tanzania

- Vertex Financial Services

For more information on the Dar es Salaam Stock Exchange please visit their website www.dse.co.tz

## Kenya and Uganda Stock Exchanges

Nairobi Stock Exchange (NSE) and Uganda Securities Exchange (USE) also have a number of listed company shares, which can be purchased through their respective licensed stockbrokers.

Nairobi Stock Exchange has a total of 46 listed companies in the following categories; Agriculture, Commercial and Services, Finance and Investment, and Industrial and Allied. There are 19 licensed stockbrokers at NSE.

For more information visit their website at www.nse.co.ke

Uganda Securities Exchange has listed 12 company shares, which can be traded through any of the 8 licensed security dealers. Investment advisor firms are also available to provided investment guidance to investors.

For more information visit their website at www.use.or.ug

**Treasury Bills and Treasury Bonds in East Africa**

Treasury Bills (T-Bills) and Treasury Bonds (T-Bonds) are government securities issued by the central bank of a country. T-Bills are short-term securities while T-Bonds are medium to long-term securities. These securities can be used as collateral against borrowing and they are generally very low risk since the government issues them.

For participation in the purchase of government securities in East Africa visit the websites of the central bank of the specific country. For convenience, the website addresses are provided at the end of this book.

The DSE also trades in Government bonds (there are 10 listed government bonds) and corporate bonds (there are 7 listed corporate bonds). CRDB bank has been licensed to buy and sell government securities such as Treasury bills and Treasury bonds. This may help encourage secondary market trading for securities.

**Mutual funds or Collective investment schemes**

A mutual fund or collective investment scheme (such as Umoja Fund or NICO Investment) is a professionally managed company that collects money from a number of investors. The mutual fund uses the collected monies to purchase company shares or stocks, bonds and other securities.

National Investment Company (NICO) uses the collected funds to purchase state owned entities that have been partially privatized or are yet to be privatized.

Collective investment schemes (mutual funds) enable individual investors to diversify thereby be able to minimize risk while affording to enjoy the benefits of good returns from a number of investment categories all at the same time.

Most Mutual funds invest in a combination of stocks/shares and bonds, including government securities.

## Real Estate (Owning a home)

Several banks currently provide their qualified customers with home loans so that they can manage to buy or build their own homes. One of the requirements is to have a job.

Azania Bank's website provides an online calculator that can be used to determine a possible repayment schedule in case you decide to take a home loan. This calculates how much will be needed each month (and for how long) in order to repay the loan.

## Some of the important factors to consider when shopping for the best home loan are:

1. Interest rate

2. Collateral needed, if any

3. Loan repayment start date

4. Fees and commissions to be paid in order to process the loan

5. The term of the loan (the length of time that is expected for you to repay the loan)

6. Default policy - what will happen to your loan or collateral in case you miss payments or are unable to repay the loan

# Saving while outside Tanzania

The Tanzanite account is an account offered at the CRDB bank and can be opened by Tanzanians while out of the country.

The Tanzanite account is designated for non-resident Tanzanians and requires a minimum of Tshs. 100,000 or USD/GBP/EUR 100. The account can be opened through the Tanzanian embassy in the customer's country of residence.

This account earns 0.5% interest above regular interest rates and the minimum balance to start earning interest is USD/GBP/EUR 500.

# Risk Management

Risk management is an important part of the investment process. All types of investment have a certain degree of risk.

**Risk tolerance level** is the degree at which you are willing to tolerate the uncertainty surrounding the safety of your investment capital. Risk tolerance levels vary among individuals.

## Factors that may affect risk tolerance levels

- **Age** – the younger you are, the higher your risk tolerance level might be. This is because you have more time to invest and minimize risk.

- **Financial goals** – the closer you are to reaching your financial goal the lower your risk tolerance level will be. This is because you would want to keep all invested funds safe in order to achieve your financial goals.

- **Income** – this can also affect how much risk you are willing to tolerate because a situation where you loose all of your investment capital will affect your financial abilities if that was all the money you were depending on.

### Risk vs. Returns

Generally less risk means less returns or rewards. Even investments that are (most of the times) deemed to be risk free such as government securities, do have some amount of risk. The risk of a rising inflation rate can reduce the real value of expected yield in government securities.

The stock market is more volatile than other investments in the short run but delivers higher returns in the long run and is therefore a good long-term investment vehicle if you are ready to be patient.

People with lower risk tolerance levels usually invest less in stocks and more in bonds while people with higher risk tolerance levels such as the younger generation (not too close to retirement age) have a longer investment time horizon so they can invest more in stocks and less in bonds.

## Ways to reduce risk

In the stock market you can be somehow certain of what will happen but betting on when it will happen could be an expensive gamble. Here are a few possible ways to reduce risk.

- **Balance your investment portfolio**. Asset Allocation or Balancing involves investing in different types of asset classes that is Cash, Stocks/Shares and Bonds. Asset Allocation or Balancing reduces market risk, for example when bonds are not doing very well then stocks and cash can be depended upon to reduce market risk.

- **Diversify your investment portfolio.** Diversifying refers to investing in many companies within the same asset class. Diversifying reduces overall portfolio risk such that when the stock of say company A is not doing well the effect is reduced by the good performance of company B etc. This is the same as not putting all your eggs in one basket.

- **Invest in mutual funds.** To minimize the possibility of choosing the wrong stock one may decide to invest in mutual funds such as the collective investment scheme Umoja Fund or National Investments Company Limited (NICO) where the mutual fund managers will make the choice for you (on your behalf). However before making any investment decisions careful considerations and thorough research needs to be done regarding the mutual funds. Most of the time there are management fees, which may reduce investment returns.

- **Focus on investing for the long haul.** Most investments fair well when they are held over long periods of time therefore it helps to start investing at an early age.

- **Choose high quality investments.** Purchasing shares of companies that show a probability of doing well in the future requires thorough research. This can be done through the use of investment advisors.

Investments will need to be monitored and evaluated at least once every year to determine their performance and whether they still meet expectations. Adjustments may be needed where necessary in order to maintain investments that still meet the established financial goals.

To get investment advice, please contact a local Investment Broker or Investment Advisor. Some brokers recommend products because they get commission therefore it is important to find an advisor who will be objective enough to provide recommendations based on what is right for you.

# Writing a Last Will

This step may not necessarily depend on other steps. It can be dealt with at the very beginning of the process because a Will needs to be reviewed at least once a year and especially after a major event such as marriage, birth of a baby or death of someone mentioned in the Will. This means a Will can be written at any stage of life and revised as the years go by.

Every independent adult especially those with children are advised to have a Last Will. The scope of this book does not cover the legal issues that are involved in how to write a Will, however this information can be obtained through any local law office.

# Advantages of writing a Last Will

It helps answer questions about your wishes in the event of your death

- Ensures that your children and/or dependents receive their rightful inheritance as you wish
- Through a Will you will also be able to appoint your preferred legal guardian for your children if you and your spouse both die before your children reach the legal adult age
- The Last Will also helps to avoid family conflicts particularly where different traditional customs are involved
- A Will also helps clarify legal issues in case your spouse is remarried

However it may be necessary to see a local attorney in your area or country in order to make sure that the Will you write is within the local legal requirements.

## Some of the contents of a Will include:

- List of children if any with their full names
- Executor of the Will (person who will carry out provisions of the Will) this can be a lawyer
- Guardian for dependent children in case both parents die at the same time
- Distribution of property
- Witnesses
- Other provisions based on individual situations

***Tip:*** All investments have some risk therefore matching financial goals with specific categories of investments may help in the selection of appropriate investments in order to accomplish established financial goals.

# STEP 6: Insurance Planning

| In summary, this chapter will cover: |
| :--- |
| - Basic insurance terms |
| - Importance of insurance coverage |
| - Insurance benefits in Tanzania |

According to the American Heritage dictionary:

**Insurance** is coverage by a contract binding a party to indemnify another against specified loss in return for premiums paid.

## Insurance Terms defined

**Insured** – this is the person who buys insurance to protect themselves from a variety of events as specified on the insurance policy that he/she holds.

**Insurer** – this is the company that sells insurance coverage to the insured with a promise to pay benefits at the end of the term or when specified event(s) occur.

**Premium** – this is amount paid (by the insured to the insurer) usually in installments for a certain amount of insurance coverage.

There are several insurance agents, insurance brokers and companies that provide advice on insurance products based on personal needs.

## Why you may need insurance coverage

- **Protect assets:** when someone owns assets there is a need to protect these assets. In case something happens to the assets and depending on the type of coverage, the insurance company pays for the loss.

- **Provide for dependants:** more importantly, one may need life insurance if they have a spouse, children and other dependents. Individuals or couples who have children or dependants are also faced with the need to seek life insurance coverage to protect their children's financial well being in the event that they die while their children are still young and completely dependant on them. With life insurance the insurance company agrees to pay a certain amount of money to beneficiaries when the insured dies. This is one way to provide financial security to dependants in the event of the death of the financial provider(s). The responsibility of the insured will be to submit payments (premiums) as agreed upon by the insurance company. The amount of premium paid depends on a variety of factors such as medical history, age, occupation and gender.

- **Supplement pension:** Life insurance is also needed if pension or savings are not enough to take care of the financial needs of dependants in the event of the insured's death.

- **Cover sources of income:** Life insurance can be bought to cover income, outstanding debt, employer benefits etc.

There are a variety of life insurance plans to buy from. Some of the plans include:

- **Term life insurance**: This will provide death benefits to your beneficiaries if you die during the term of the policy. The term is usually a specified time period of say 30 years.

- **Whole life insurance**: This provides protection and over time cash value is built up with the premiums remaining at a fixed amount for the duration of the contract. You can withdraw cash or borrow against the cash value of the policy.

# Basic insurance classes

- Temporary
- Permanent

## Temporary/Term life insurance

- Provides life insurance for a specified number of years and for a specific premium
- It is considered "pure" insurance because by paying the premium the insured gets protection in the event of death only
- Policy does not accumulate cash value

**To purchase term life insurance one needs to consider the following:**

- The cost to be incurred in terms of premium payments
- Length of coverage (term)
- Face amount (Death benefit)

**What it means:**

If the insured or policyholder dies before the term is up, the beneficiaries receive a death benefit, however if the insured does not die and the term is up nothing is received. Death by suicide is usually excluded if it can be proven that the suicide was intentional in order to receive the benefits.

## Permanent Life Insurance

- This is life insurance that remains in place until the policy pays out except when premiums are not paid when due
- Builds cash value
- The owner/insured can withdraw the money, borrow the cash value or surrender the policy and get the surrender value
- The policy cannot be cancelled by the insurer (insurance company)

**What it means:**

The insured or policyholder can benefit from the cash value while still alive and the beneficiaries will obtain the death benefits in the event of the insured's death.

**Three types of permanent life insurance**

- Whole life
- Universal life
- Endowment

**Whole life**

- Has fixed and known annual premiums, not flexible
- Offers guaranteed death benefits
- Offers guaranteed cash values
- Premiums may be higher when compared to term insurance, but only in the short term
- Mortality and expense charges do not reduce the cash value in the policy
- Internal rate of return may not be as competitive as other savings options

**Universal life**

- Includes a cash account which is increased by premiums
- Mortality charges and other administrative costs reduce the cash account
- Interest is paid within the policy and credited to the account
- Greater flexibility in premiums
- Higher internal rate of return
- Surrender value is the amount remaining on the cash account after charges

### Endowment

- Premium paying period is shortened and the endowment date is earlier compared to other types of insurance which makes premiums more expensive
- Endowment insurance is paid out after a specified period or age, whether the insured dies or lives
- Cash value is built up inside the policy
- Cash value equals the death benefit at a certain age

# Insurance benefits in Tanzania

Several insurance companies in Tanzania offer policies that cover a variety of areas. The National Insurance Company (NIC) has been offering these policies for a number of years however; there are other insurance companies that offer similar or slightly different policy coverage. The important thing is to find out more information and make a decision based on individual needs.

Examples of these policies are discussed below.

## Super Education Provider

Super Education Provider is designed to provide parents with financial support for their children's education.

There are 4 options provided by the NIC Tanzania.

Option 1: Kinder Super Education Provider covering Primary School Education fees.

Option 2: Junior Super Education Provider covering Secondary School Education fees.

Option 3: Senior Super Education Provider covering University Education expenses.

Option 4: Combination of option 2 and option 3.

## Super Life Provider

This is Life insurance policy that provides benefits to you (the insured) during your retirement years. In case you die prematurely, the policy pays benefits to your dependents supporting them on the financial loss they may suffer as a result of your death.

## Pensave Scheme

This is a retirement savings program provided by the National Insurance Corporation of Tanzania. The Pensave plan gives flexibility on contributions; you decide when you want to contribute and how much. The plan also allows you to take the savings with you as you move from one employer to another during your working years.


Several other types of policies are offered, for more information visit the NIC website directly at www.nictanzania.com and click on Products & Services.


***Tip:*** Not everyone needs all types of insurance coverage therefore it is important to review personal insurance needs and determine whether it is necessary to obtain coverage.

# STEP 7: Retirement Planning

**In summary, this chapter will cover:**

- Factors that affect availability of retirement income

- Management of an effective retirement plan

- When to start saving for retirement

Retirement planning involves setting aside money for retirement years. This could be the only money available at retirement or it could be supplemented by income earned after retirement years since sometimes people continue to work after the official retirement for a number of reasons. In most cases income obtained from pension funds or 401 (k) plans is not enough to take care of all financial needs at retirement.

With a continuous flow of income at retirement it is also possible to pursue activities of interest that were not possible to pursue while working.

Financial advisors recommend that an average person will need approximately 70% of pre-retirement income to maintain the same standard of living after they stop working. Also, an average person will likely spend about one third (1/3) of their life in retirement.

## Why save for retirement?

- **We don't know how long we will live** – If we live longer than expected and retirement money does not last that long it may lead to insufficient funds.

- **We don't know for how long we will be able to work** – It is common for people to retire earlier than expected as a result of health problems or being laid off from the company they worked for.

- **To have enough funds for a comfortable retirement** – Unfortunately the amount of money contributed by the employer for retirement is never enough during retirement. The assumption that expenses will go down during retirement is not usually true and if inflation is taken into consideration, it means more money will be needed. In addition, other expenses may arise, such as providing financial help for dependant children or grandchildren and parents, increased medical costs and rising health insurance premium costs.

## Factors that may affect how much money is available at retirement

- **Paying for children's education** - Paying for children's education expenses (college education) may greatly reduce the funds available for saving and investing for retirement.

- **Time** - Starting to save and invest early in a career provides a great head start. The more time there is from when someone starts to save for retirement to the time they retire, the more funds will likely be available, assuming everything else remains constant.

- **Rate of return** – Selecting an investment with a higher rate of return increases funds available at retirement. It is important to remember that higher rates of return mean a higher investment risk. The tradeoff in this case is that when the retirement date is still far away it is possible to take more risk. The best way to minimize investment risk and maximize investment returns is to diversify the investment portfolio.

- **Contribution amount** – The amount that each employee contributes to supplement what the employer provides makes a difference on how much money will be available after retirement. Supplemental retirement money can be invested through the supplemental retirement program available where the employer contributions are sent such as the PPF (Parastatal Pension Fund) fund or NSSF (National Social Security Fund) or other investment firms based on country of residence.

# When and how to start saving for retirement

- **Start planning for retirement now** - Experts recommend to start saving for retirement as early as possible. In this case it makes sense to start saving for Retirement on the same month that Employment begins.

- **Set aside a specified percentage of income** - If every month a certain specified percentage of income no matter how small, is set aside and then invested it will accumulate over the years. The best way is always to do so before other expenses start coming in because then it will be more difficult to try and keep from spending that money. If it is possible, open an account with a bank that will allow direct deposit of money from the employer. This way you will not "see" the money being set aside.

- **Keep it up** - Consistency is another key to a successful retirement savings plan. No matter how hard it gets, regular savings for retirement should be kept going. Exceptions can be made but what is important is to maintain the discipline.

- **Find information about available options** - There are currently a number of options that are fit for retirement savings. It is important to do research to find out which options are right for you.

# How to manage a retirement plan

### When young and far from retirement consider focusing on:

- High yield investments (these are likely to be more risky)
- Hold long-term investments to take advantage of long term returns and minimize fluctuations in prices
- Growth investments that will increase the value of investment with time
- Investments such as more company shares/stocks and less in bonds

### When getting closer to retirement consider moving funds to:

- Less risky investments
- Income generating investments
- Short term investments
- Investments such as more bonds/securities and less shares/stocks
- Gradually start to move funds to highly liquid investments

### During retirement consider finalizing Retirement Planning:

- Opt for investments with 100% guarantee of principal
- Choose investments with much shorter maturity. Spread the maturity dates of investments so that with each investment's maturity date there is a continuous flow of income such as monthly or every 3 months. An example would be Fixed deposit accounts that mature say in March, June, September and December of every year and so on.
- Move to investment vehicles such as short term bonds and Fixed Deposits

# Current global market conditions

The United States and the global financial markets are currently experiencing significant turbulence and retirement accounts have lost large amounts of money. The question of how much loss one person might incur depends largely on how they invested (diversified) and how long it will be before they need the money. This is because the loss is not really incurred until one decides to cash out of their retirement plan. The stock market will very likely recover and those who ride out the storm (since patience pays) will reap the benefits if and when things return to normal. Again, this depends on how long it is before someone retires.

# Retirement plans

Retirement planning (saving) can be accomplished through a variety of steps all of which are recommended for every employee.

- Basic and mandatory contributions through employers (contributed by employee and employer)
- Supplemental contributions which are more flexible
- Investing in long term investment vehicles such as government securities when the investor is young and far from retirement (or a combination of government securities and stocks/company shares depending on the investor's risk tolerance level) or investing in more liquid investments such as fixed deposits for an investor who is closer to retirement.

In the next section we will discuss retirement plans as offered by the Parastatal Pension Fund (PPF) in Tanzania, as an example of available options.

## Basic and mandatory contributions

Contribution rates:

- 5% for employee and 15% for employer
- 10% for employee and 10% for employer

Employers are required by law to submit their share of contribution and the contributions deducted from their employees' salaries.

## Supplemental contributions

Employees who contribute to a basic and mandatory social security fund can also contribute into a supplemental scheme. Since the basic contribution is usually not sufficient to cover all financial needs during retirement it is strongly recommended that employees contribute to a supplemental scheme after fulfilling the mandatory requirements. The employee alone or employer alone or both employee and employer can make contributions. Financial planning experts recommend maximizing the amount that you can possibly contribute in the supplemental scheme.

A member decides upon contribution rates in a supplemental scheme as follows:

- Percentage of income
- Fixed amount
- Combination of percentage of income or fixed amount

Benefits that can be obtained under a pension fund such as PPF (Parastatal Pension Fund) are as follows:

- Education benefits - up to 4 children of a member who dies while in service can be granted funds for school expenses from nursery to ordinary secondary school level

- Withdrawal benefits - lump sum total of employee's and employer's contribution in case an employee terminates employment or as a result of a summary dismissal (being fired)
- Disability benefits - depending on length of contributing period, disability benefits are granted when a member ceases employment on medical grounds per the Medical Board's recommendation
- Gratuity benefits - (less than 10 years contributing period) Gratuity benefits paid to employee as a result of retirement in public interest, retrenchment (layoff) or removal by Presidential decree
- Survivor benefits - benefits granted to dependants (wife, husband, children or parents of member) where a member dies while in service after at least 10 years contributing period
- Death benefits - depending on length of contributing period, a lump sum amount is paid to deceased member's legal person representative
- Old age benefits - (after at least 10 years contributing period) when a member ceases employment after reaching retirement age, retirement in public interest, retrenchment (layoff) or removal from employment by Presidential decree or any other authority at retirement age

# Retirement saving through regular investments or individual retirement account

In addition to the basic and supplemental contributions, retirement planning can also be done through personal investment in government securities (in case of a long investment time horizon) or fixed deposits (in case of a short investment time horizon).

**Investment time horizon** is the length of time an individual needs from the point when they start saving for a particular financial goal to the point when they need to fulfill that particular financial goal. For example if Halima starts working and saving for retirement at age 25 and expects to retire at age 55 then Halima's investment time horizon is 30 years. On the other hand if John starts working at age 25 but starts saving for retirement at age 45 while also expecting to retire at age 55 then John's investment time horizon is only 10 years.

Apart from investment time horizon the choice of an appropriate investment for retirement saving also depends on an individual's risk tolerance level. An individual with a low risk tolerance is likely to avoid investments that he or she considers to be too risky. However it is also important to remember that risk and return move in the same direction therefore the riskier an investment is the more likely it is to have higher returns.

In any case, saving for retirement or any other financial goal will be more successful if started early. It is better to start saving with the smallest amount possible than not to start at all or to wait until there is extra money.

# Funding an Individual Retirement Account

Below are examples of how an early start can make a significant difference as far as how much is needed to fund an individual retirement account. These calculations can be done using a simple financial calculator such as Hewlett-Packard HB 10B-II model, which provides instructions for its function keys.

## Assumptions made:

- These calculations have not been adjusted to take into account the expected rate of inflation, which may cause the monthly contribution needed to exceed what has been reflected in the examples below.

- Monthly salary remained the same throughout the person's life.

- For simplicity, the monthly salary is the same for all examples.

- There are no other retirement earnings or the amount is too small to make a difference and therefore individual retirement savings contributions are the only option.

**Example 1:** Monthly contributions that start at age 25 and continue into age 65.

| Description | Value |
|---|---|
| Current age - in years | 25 |
| Age at retirement - in years | 65 |
| Investment horizon (time available) - in years | 40 |
| Length of time in which income will be needed | 30 |
| Current monthly salary | 100,000 |
| Current annual salary | 1,200,000 |
| Income needed at retirement - 70% of current annual income | 840,000 |
| Value of investment at time of retirement | 25,200,000 |
| Expected interest rate | 6% |
| **Monthly savings amount needed to reach retirement goal** | **13,569** |
| **Monthly savings amount as a percentage of monthly salary** | **14%** |

**Example 2:** Monthly contributions that start at age 35 and continue into age 65.

| Description | Value |
|---|---|
| Current age - in years | 35 |
| Age at retirement - in years | 65 |
| Investment horizon (time available) - in years | 30 |
| Length of time in which income will be needed | 30 |
| Current monthly salary | 100,000 |
| Current annual salary | 1,200,000 |
| Income needed at retirement - 70% of current annual income | 840,000 |
| Value of investment at time of retirement | 25,200,000 |
| Expected interest rate | 6% |
| **Monthly savings amount needed to reach retirement goal** | **26,563** |
| **Monthly savings amount as a percentage of monthly salary** | **27%** |

**Example 3:** Monthly contributions that start at age 45 and continue into age 65.

| Description | Value |
|---|---|
| Current age - in years | 45 |
| Age at retirement - in years | 65 |
| Investment horizon (time available) - in years | 20 |
| Length of time in which income will be needed | 30 |
| Current monthly salary | 100,000 |
| Current annual salary | 1,200,000 |
| Income needed at retirement - 70% of current annual income | 840,000 |
| Value of investment at time of retirement | 25,200,000 |
| Expected interest rate | 6% |
| **Monthly savings amount needed to reach retirement goal** | **57,088** |
| **Monthly savings amount as a percentage of monthly salary** | **57%** |

**Example 4:** Monthly contributions that start at age 55 and continue into age 65.

| Description | Value |
|---|---|
| Current age - in years | 55 |
| Age at retirement - in years | 65 |
| Investment horizon (time available) - in years | 10 |
| Length of time in which income will be needed | 30 |
| Current monthly salary | 100,000 |
| Current annual salary | 1,200,000 |
| Income needed at retirement - 70% of current annual income | 840,000 |
| Value of investment at time of retirement | 25,200,000 |
| Expected interest rate | 6% |
| **Monthly savings amount needed to reach retirement goal** | **159,322.71** |
| **Monthly savings amount as a percentage of monthly salary** | **159%** |

**Example 5:** Monthly contributions that start at age 60 and continue into age 65.

| Description | Value |
|---|---|
| Current age - in years | 60 |
| Age at retirement - in years | 65 |
| Investment horizon (time available) - in years | 5 |
| Length of time in which income will be needed | 30 |
| Current monthly salary | 100,000 |
| Current annual salary | 1,200,000 |
| Income needed at retirement - 70% of current annual income | 840,000 |
| Value of investment at time of retirement | 25,200,000 |
| Expected interest rate | 6% |
| **Monthly savings amount needed to reach retirement goal** | **372,532** |
| **Monthly savings amount as a percentage of monthly salary** | **372%** |

In summary, based on the simple examples above, as retirement age nears the percentage of income needed to save for retirement becomes significantly larger than at a much younger age. Therefore, if individual retirement savings start past the age of 45 years, additional savings from sources other than the monthly salary will be needed to reach the retirement goal of 70% of current income since the amount needed is either above 50% of income or may result into a negative income.

***Tip:*** The younger we are the better it is to start saving for retirement, however in practice, the more difficult it is to actually do it on a consistent basis and that is why an effective retirement plan is necessary.

# STEP 8: Saving for kids' education

| **In summary, this chapter will cover:** |
| --- |
| - When to start saving for children's education |
| - How to manage a college savings plan |
| - Children's bank accounts |

Saving for kids education can be started as early as when the child celebrates his/her first birthday. This way there will be enough time to establish strategies or change strategies when the need arises. For example if you start saving for your 2 year old child so that she/he can go to college when she/he is 18, there would be about 16 years to accumulate savings to pay for college expenses.

Saving for kids' education may include saving for primary education, secondary/high school and college education.

## Factors to consider when managing a college savings plan

- It is important to know the expected college fees in order to find out how much needs to be saved in the time frame that is available. Therefore, find out more information about different university colleges, what degrees they offer and how much they charge for their programs so as to get an idea of how much will be needed.

- Another important aspect for consideration is high inflation rates and how that can affect accumulated savings.

- Recommended investment vehicles for college savings would include company shares and bonds so as to invest for the long run (10 – 15 years). As the child gets close to joining college (say 5 years before) funds may be moved into safer and more liquid accounts such as Fixed Deposit to ensure guaranteed payout when the money is needed.

- Tax implications should be taken into consideration at all times. For example shares traded through the Dar es Salaam Stock Exchange are either exempted from some types of tax or in other cases the tax rate is lower compared to unlisted equities.

Parents can open bank accounts as early as when their children are born, and continue to deposit money into the accounts over the years even when only small amounts can be afforded. It may be a good idea to open at least 2 accounts per child. One account can be for their education expenses and the other account for transferring to the child once they are old enough to maintain it on their own. Once the child reaches the appropriate age, parents can transfer ownership of this account to the child in order to start providing the child with a sense of financial independence, accountability and responsibility. With hands on approach, children will learn how and where to save their earnings (regardless of amount) while they are still under the support of their parents. Parents can continue to save for their children through both accounts.

There are a few banks that provide savings account options for parents and/or guardians to start saving for their children's education or other financial needs and to help teach children how to manage their money and cultivate a savings culture.

# Examples of bank accounts for children:

Nyota Children's Plan at Exim bank allows for monthly savings of a fixed deposit in the names of children who are under 18 years of age, with a minimum balance of Tshs. 10,000. Parents can make deposits for a specific term of 3, 5 or 7 years.

For more information visit their website at www.eximbank-tz.com

At CRDB bank, the Junior Jumbo account is offered with an opening amount of Tshs. 20,000 or 20 USD/EURO/GBP for children under the age of 18 years. Holders of this account enjoy higher interest rates than normal savings account holders for balances that are equal to or above Tshs. 100,000 or 500 USD/EURO/GBP. A bonus interest of 0.5% per year is awarded to accounts that maintain balances of Tshs. 5,000,000 throughout the year. After the child turns 18 years old, the account can be changed to a normal savings account.

For more information visit their website at www.crdbbank.com

The School Savings Account at the National Microfinance Bank (NMB) is designed specifically to help parents save for their children's education. Only parents are authorized to operate this account and a minimum of Tshs. 10,000 for 2 years is required. Withdrawals are only allowed through direct payments to schools.

For more information visit their website at www.nmbtz.cpom

Akiba Commercial Bank (T) provides Zawadi Account for children below 18 years of age. The account allows for parents and guardians to save for educational purposes and other needs for their children. The opening amount is Tshs. 5,000 and withdrawals are limited to four times a year if the minimum balance of Tshs. 20,000 is maintained at all times.

For more information visit their website at www.acb-bank.com

The Cub accounts at Kenya Commercial Bank (T) is available for parents to save for their children's needs and includes a free Bankers check for every school term to take care of educational needs.

For more information visit their website at www.kcbbankgroup.com/tz/index.php

Over the years, the Postal Bank savings account had been one of the accounts opened by most parents for their children.

Most of these savings accounts for children earn interest; however, some may have minimum balance requirements in order to earn interest. Most of them do not have any charges, however it is always important to visit the local bank branch or their website so as to obtain up-to-date information and make an educated decision.

***Tip:*** The best inheritance we can provide for our children is a good education and that will be money well spent.

# STEP 9: Starting a business

| In summary, this chapter will cover: |
| :--- |
| - Basics of starting, funding and managing a business |
| - Qualities of an entrepreneur |
| - Starting and managing an online business |
| - Analysis of costs associated with online businesses |

Starting a business can be exciting and challenging. There are several issues that may need to be sorted out and decided upon before starting any business.

## What to know before starting any business

### 1. How do you want to start your business?

There are several ways to start a business:

- Develop an idea, obtain funding and establish a new company

- Buy an existing business and run it yourself

- Purchase a franchise that has already been established with a recognizable product, existing supply network and pre-established business procedures

- Become an independent consultant

## 2. Business Structure and business name

The business name and structure can be based on the nature of the business and how many people will be involved in running it.

- Sole Proprietorship

- Partnership

- Company

## 3. Legal issues

Find out what local legal procedures need to be followed in order to start a business.

Some of the requirements include:

- Licensing

- Permit

- Registration

## 4. Tax requirements

Determine what the local and government tax system is and how it affects your business.

Some requirements may include:

- Knowing what taxes your business will be required to pay, such as value added tax, property tax, income tax, sales tax

- In some countries, there is a need to find out how your accounting system will affect your tax filing

- Filing for a federal tax identification number (in the USA)

## 5. Financing and budgeting

It is important to have a budget that can be used to keep the business on track and monitor expenses. Financing can be obtained from a number of sources including:

- Personal savings – using personal savings to finance the business

- Borrowing money - from family, friends or colleague at an agreed rate and terms

- Getting a loan from the bank – apply for a business loan from the bank (which will require a business plan to be submitted)

## 6. Accounting

A decision will need to be made regarding accounting and bookkeeping issues. Various choices can be made such as:

- In-house or outsource – this will involve whether to have someone outside your business do your accounting or to hire an in-house bookkeeper

- Accounting software – this will help minimize accounting errors and simplify the bookkeeping process while providing important financial reports that are crucial in making important decisions for the business. Accounting software include QuickBooks, Peachtree

- Accounting system – accrual or cash method

## 7. Staffing needs

Based on the type of business you are running, determine how customers will be served. A few options are available:

- Hire employees

- Find a business partner

- Work alone

## 8. Business plan

Write-up a business plan that can be used to:

- Obtain financing from the bank

- Provide structure for the business

- Monitor and evaluate performance of the business

- Provide direction and help foresee the future

## 9. Marketing

A marketing plan will include strategies, type of media to be used, cost and target market among other things. Some of the ways to market your business include:

- Press release

- Online advertising such as pay-per-click (Google, Yahoo etc)

- Craigslist

- Buyerzone

- sba.org (in the US)

- Yellow pages

- Local newspapers

- Referral discounts

- Coupons and other freebies

- Fliers, posters and business cards

- Direct mailing

- Email marketing

### 10. Resources

Determine where to obtain useful resources for running the business and for future advancement:

- Books – these can be purchased or borrowed from a library.

- Internet – spend time searching the internet for information, subscribe to online newsletters.

- Networking – use networking gatherings to exchange ideas with other businessmen and women.

- Seminars, workshops and conferences – register and attend seminars etc hosted by experts in your field.

- Magazine subscriptions – subscribe to print or online magazines and get updates on new trends in the industry the business belongs to.

# Qualities of an entrepreneur

Below are some of the qualities:

- Strong inner drive to succeed
- Competitive by nature
- Risk taker
- Continuous learner
- Able to accept constructive criticism
- Highly self-disciplined
- Ability to work extra hours above the regular business hours
- Self motivated
- Confident
- Able to initiate something and see it through to the end without giving up
- A good leader

- A good money manager
- Open to change

## Advantages of operating your own business

- Being your own boss
- Doing something you personally like
- The possibility of making more income

## Disadvantages of operating your own business

- If there is a business loss you are the one to bear it
- Most of the time you may need to work extra hours to keep the business going
- Lack of financial self discipline is likely to cause the business financial trouble

## Funding the business

Raising capital for a business is a challenging task but can be accomplished in a variety of ways. Capital can be obtained through personal savings, borrowing from family and friends or borrowing from financial institutions such as a bank or SACCO.

**SACCO** is the acronym for **S**avings **A**nd **C**redit **Co**-operative. SACCO is basically the same as a Credit Union which is a name used in other countries. A Savings and Credit Co-operative is owned, governed and managed by its members who usually have the same common bond such as working for the same employer or living in the same community. Members agree to save their money together in the SACCO and they agree to make loans to each other at reasonable rates of interest.

# Things to consider before obtaining a business loan

- A business plan will be needed. Free samples are available on the Internet. Depending on the size of the loan, it may be important to search for the services of a consultant in order to get professional guidance on how to write a business plan.

- Establish a strategy for repayment of the loan especially how to pay it on time so as to reduce or eliminate extra fees, which may in turn decrease profits for the business. Avoid defaulting on the loan by being prepared and planning ahead.

- Ensure that the loan money is used strictly for the intended business and not for personal expenses.

- Read all loan documents carefully and do not hesitate to ask questions if there is an area that is not clear.

- Keep accurate and up-to-date books of records for the business to ensure proper money management. This can be accomplished through appropriate accounting software, an organized filing system and a computer or by using book-keeping books.

# Financial Leasing

Financial Leasing is a medium-term financial instrument for the purchase of equipment, properties and vehicles.

Financial Leasing according to the Tanzania Leasing Project (TANZALEP) newsletter issue # 01 (June – September 2005), is an alternative to traditional long-term bank loans. The difference stems from the fact that unlike traditional loans, leasing will be beneficial to small and medium businesses that do not have collateral, which is a requirement in most traditional loans.

Currently, TANZALEP produces a Financial Leasing Newsletter (issued quarterly) that is being featured on the National Website.

## Go global

There are a lot of businesses that operate not just locally but rather reach out to customers around the world. Some of the businesses are operated entirely through the Internet without a brick and mortar location and this means that online business skills are becoming increasingly vital. Most businesses are establishing their web presence through unique domain names and creation of websites, web logs and discussion forums or chat in order to expand their customer base or stay in touch with customers 365 days of the year.

## Hobbies

Exploring hobbies and finding ways to make some extra money may bring some extra cash flow. Sometimes these activities may become the main income sources through self-employment. Hobbies such as writing, drawing, painting, carpentry, construction, interior design, sewing, knitting, catering/cooking etc. could provide some extra money for an individual or family.

Hobbies are also a good way to relax after a long day at work, therefore making extra income out of hobbies can provide even more satisfaction. It is important to do thorough research on possible markets and to find out how much capital will be needed to start with.

## How to keep a new business moving forward

Maintaining growth for a new business is one of the most challenging tasks for new business owners. Here are a few tips to make it possible.

- **Set a big vision** – Aim high even if you start low this helps set the tone for the business and the quality of product or service to be offered.

- **Make decisions quickly** – Other companies are already moving forward, a startup in its early stages needs to catch up and the timing for decision-making may make all the difference.

- **Give customers a reason to keep coming back** – always aim at retaining customers not just attracting new ones. Loyal customers are great contributors to successful business.

- **Deliver more than you promise** – give customers a chance to see the business exceed expectations, it will keep them wanting more of the product or service.

- **Urgency is important in everything you do** – whatever can be done now or today needs to be done rather than postponed.

- **Do not spend more money than you have to** – avoid spending more than necessary and save the money for more crucial expenses.

- **Hire people who know what they are doing** – it is better to hire a few people who are good rather than many who may not be very competent.

- **Learn to sell** – rather than expecting the sales personnel to do all the selling be sure to get to know the process too.

- **Operate at a profit for the products/services** – profits will keep the business going, big companies have the advantage of volume even when they minimize the profit margin, startups don't.

- **Implement the marketing strategy diligently** - marketing is what will bring the product/service to the customers this may include word of mouth, referral bonuses, press releases, newsletters etc.

# Starting an online business

There are a number of ways to earn income online, some of them include:

1. **Google Adsense** – this is the most common way to earn income online. Write and publish valuable content, put Google advertisements on your website or blog. When visitors surf the website in search of information, they may click on relevant advertisements to get more information. Get paid for all these clicks. There are several ways to earn money through Google: Content, Search, Referrals, Video Links and more. Visit Google and search for "Google Adsense". Registration is free.

2. **Become a reseller** – A reseller purchases hosting plans, domains, blogs, e-commerce products and other web products at a wholesale price (lower than normal retail prices) and resells these products to others at prices set by him/her. This gives the reseller the flexibility of determining how much profit they would like to make. Some of the best wholesale rates can be found at www.neptunewebservices.com. Click on the link for Resellers.

3. **Affiliate programs** –Include links from other websites that provide affiliate programs, drive traffic to these affiliate websites and earn money when someone buys their products. Some of the most popular ones are Amazon.com and Ebay.com. Go to www.amazon.com and www.ebay.com and at the bottom click on the link Join Associates or Affiliates (respectively) and follow instructions.

4. **Become a published author** – write and publish books on your topic of interest then sell them through print or electronically. One such website where it is possible to publish and sell books is www.lulu.com or www.createspace.com. Also, at www.authorsden.com a community of authors and readers, authors can market their books, published and unpublished works to their

intended audience. Be sure to copyright your materials so that your efforts are not in vain.

5. **Sell merchandise or services online** – Identify products or services that might have a potential market then do some research online and offline to find suppliers while paying attention to the business laws in your country of residence. Purchase an e-commerce website and domain name that identifies your business. At www.neptunewebservices.com there are ready to use templates (2 in 1 package of hosting and shopping cart software known as Quick Shopping Cart) that can be customized to individual preferences and fits any level of web design experience, advanced or beginner. Your online store will be up and running in a matter of minutes. For businesses that offer services, a regular hosting plan for a website and a domain registration may provide a good start for finding clients online (these can also be purchased at www.neptunewebservices.com).

6. **Advertisements** – once your website/blog is well known and there are a lot of visitors/traffic, companies may be willing to advertise directly through your site therefore generating the site more income.

Start with one income stream and upgrade to multiple income streams as it feels comfortable and as experience and time allow.

There are several companies that register domain names and provide web-hosting services. I use Neptune Web Services for domain and web hosting needs.

As such in the next few sections we will discuss examples of services provided at www.neptunewebservices.com.

# Be a reseller of web products

Neptune Web Services offers 2 reseller plans, Basic and Pro.

### What is included in the reseller plans?

The following are some of the benefits that come with the purchase of any of the 2 plans:

- **A storefront ready to go live within minutes** - this can be customized, to individual preferences and once published it can be shared with friends, colleagues, co-workers, clients and the world. This means profits can start to be earned immediately after purchasing the reseller plan.

- **A "Getting started guide"** - available after logging in to the reseller account

- **A "How to be a reseller" e-book** - available after logging in to the reseller account.

- **Access to Press Release templates** - these are prepared templates that can be used as your own to let the world know of the products that your business is offering.

- **Access to reseller discussion forums** - these have a wealth of information from veteran resellers and provide an opportunity for new resellers to ask questions about their business and find quick solutions.

- **Access to newsletters** - these provide continued updates on issues of importance to resellers and their customers.

Either way, the reseller even though new to the business, is able to find valuable information at their fingertips to help them run their business in a profitable and exciting way.

## What products are available to Resellers?

At Neptune Web Services both Basic and Pro reseller plans allow resellers to provide the following products to their customers:

- Domains and related products

- Hosting and related products

- Email and related products

- Website builders and tools

- Secure transactions and e-commerce solutions

## Added advantages of Pro compared to Basic Reseller

- Earn extra income with your customer's Parked domains - A Pro reseller gets 80% of revenue obtained from ads placed on customer's parked domains.

- Increase the profit margin – Be eligible for the best buy rates available. A Pro reseller gets the privilege of getting the best purchase/wholesale prices and therefore this increases the Pro reseller's profits compared to the Basic reseller. However one can always start with the Basic reseller plan and upgrade to the Pro reseller plan at any time.

- Get more credits for Google Adwords and Microsoft Adcenter promotions and get a jump-start on the marketing campaign for your business. Both Basic and Pro clients get credits for advertising, however Pro resellers get more credits compared to Basic resellers.

See a simple comparison between Basic and Pro reseller plans at www.neptunewebservices.com click on the link for Resellers. Click on "Learn more" under either of the plans and then hit the "Compare Plans" tab to get a comparison of the plans' features.

# Getting a hosting plan and a domain name

There are several options to create a web presence. Neptune Web Services guarantees 99.9% up time, which is very important when looking to earn income from a website or blog because this ensures that there will be minimal or no loss of revenue caused by downtime.

Neptune Web Services also offers products such as Web site hosting, Blog, Podcast, Spam free Emails, Reseller Plans, SSL certificates, E-Commerce solutions, dedicated servers and many more depending on particular needs. They also provide a product called Web Site Tonight (with templates) which can be used to avoid creating the website from scratch.

Neptune provides customer support 24 hours a day, 7 days a week.

# What is a Web site

Essentially, a Web site is a way to present your business online. Your Web site is a place on the Internet where anyone in the world can visit whenever they want to find out more about you, ask you questions, give you feedback, or even buy your products.

### Why do I need a Web site?

People are using the Web for everything these days. It's fast, and easy. People who prefer to shop off-line also search for product information on the Web. When people are trying to find you, the first place they look is on the Web - and if they don't find you, they will probably find someone else!

# What is a Domain Name

Your Domain Name is your address on the Web. Just like people use your phone number to call you on the phone, your Domain Name allows people to access your site on the Web. Clever, simple, or easy to remember Domain Names are most desirable as they can play a large part in attracting visitors to your site. Most Domain Names end with .com (such as tanzaniafinancials.com), but other extensions such as .net and .org are also available. In addition Domains can be used with your e-mail accounts allowing you to send and receive e-mail with addresses such as "info@yourcompany.com"

### Why purchase a domain name?

Both the Basic and Pro reseller plans have complete web addresses that start working immediately after clicking the "Go Live" button. However in order to make the storefront stand out and look unique in the web it is recommended to purchase a domain name to use along with the provided storefront. This means customers will be able to easily identify your storefront using the unique domain name associated with it.

### Additional benefits of purchasing a domain name

Several other benefits come with the purchase of a domain name. At Neptune Web Services every domain name purchase comes with the following free items:

- Email

- Blog

- Hosting

- Domain forwarding

- Domain name locking

- For Sale/Parked page

- Starter web page

- Online photo filer and many more

## How to select the right domain name for your online business

Choosing a domain name is crucial because that is the name that clients will most likely identify you with and use to refer your website to others.

Take some time to think and list down a number of domain names that sound right and start eliminating the ones that may not get your website the results you are looking for. Once the list gets to say 4 or 5 domain names, search to find out if they are available. Go to www.neptunewebservices.com to search for availability of the domain names on the list. If they are not available try using one from the alternate lists provided on the search results. If the names on the list are available, narrow down the list to the one name that is likely to bring the best results.

## Consider these tips when choosing the domain for your business:

- **Make it short and easy to remember** – once your customers know you and the products or services offered, they will likely recommend the website to friends, relatives or their clients. It will be easier for them to do so if your domain name is short and easy to remember even when someone is not able to write it down right away.

- **Include keywords** – using keywords in your domain name will increase the chances of your website being found through search engines. This may be one of the best ways to establish your online presence.

- **First buy the .com extension** – most people identify websites with the .com extension. Consider obtaining the .com extension first since most web surfers would first assume your domain name is followed by the .com extension.

- **Buy variations** – since it is also possible for competitors to purchase domain names similar to yours in an effort to divert potential customers away from your website consider purchasing variations of your business name especially if your business name has a short and long version. Once your online business is well established you may want to purchase additional extensions so that no one else can take advantage of the fruits of your hard work. To purchase additional domain extensions of .net and .org you can go to www.neptunewebservices.com.

- **You may use your given name** – This may be particularly important once your identity has been established especially to ensure that no one else purchases it before you do and uses the goodwill you have spent so much time establishing.

# What is a Blog?

'A blog is a website in which items are posted on a regular basis and displayed in reverse chronological order. The term blog is a shortened form of weblog or web log. Authoring a blog, maintaining a blog or adding an article to an existing blog is called "blogging". Individual articles on a blog are called "blog posts," "posts" or "entries". A person who posts these entries is called a "blogger". A blog comprises text, hypertext, images, and links (to other web pages and to video, audio and other files). Blogs use a conversational style of documentation. Often blogs focus on a particular "area of interest", such as politics, culture, travel or personal experiences.

# What is a podcast?

A podcast is an audio or video recording and is similar to a blog in providing a series of entries. Anyone can create a podcast. All over the world, people are creating podcasts on subjects ranging from movies, technology, music and politics, to many others. This is new original content made by passionate people who want to share their creativity with the world.

The cost to start podcasting is so low that anyone can do it.

| Sample analysis of cost and revenue for online businesses | | | |
|---|---|---|---|
| **Type of income** | **Description** | **Lowest Startup Cost \*\*\*** | **Expected revenue/profit** |
| | | Pricing examples from Neptune Web services | |
| Google adsense | Earn revenue by placing Google PPC (pay-per-click) advertisements on the website or blog. | Hosting plan as low as $3.99/mo | There is no limit to how much can be earned it all depends on clicks from visitors |
| | | Blog plan as low as $2.99/mo | |
| | | Podcast plan as low as $9.99/mo | |
| | | Domain name $3.99/yr* | |
| Reseller | Become a reseller by selling a number of products. A website/storefront is provided with the plan | Basic reseller plan $79.99/yr | Set up the price and choose products to sell and your Storefront will go live in a matter of minutes |
| | | Pro reseller plan $179.99/yr | |
| | | Domain name $3.99/yr* | |
| Affiliate programs | Write reviews for products on your website or blog and convince visitors to buy these products | Hosting plan as low as $3.99/mo | Depends on reviews written and the number of visitors for the website or blog to purchase the products |
| | | Blog plan as low as $2.99/mo | |
| | | Podcast plan as low as $9.99/mo | |
| | | Domain name $3.99/yr* | |
| Book publishing | Publish books online and sell them through a personal website or through online booksellers | The cost of purchasing a domain and hosting. However this may not be necessary if using online marketplaces such as www.lulu.com | Set the price for the books, market and then sell them. |
| Advertisements | Publish a website, add valuable content and once the website is popular companies may want to place their advertisements | Hosting plan as low as $3.99/mo | The website owner sets the price |
| | | Blog plan as low as $2.99/mo | |
| | | Podcast plan as low as $9.99/mo | |
| | | Domain name $3.99/yr* | |
| * Domain discount is offered with the purchase of a non-domain product. Regular domain price is $7.99/yr | | | |
| \*\*\* Startup cost information does not include the cost of internet access | | | |

## Create valuable content

Other ways to earn income online include writing about topics of interest. What is your passion? What knowledge, experience, expertise or education do you have that you can share with others? Start a website that will provide this information either for free or at a reasonable charge and use it to earn income. Most readers will be more interested in reading free material before they can trust the author enough to buy their products.

Valuable content can be sold as a product on its own or as a supplement to other tangible products that are being sold online. For example if someone is in the business of selling computers they may provide their visitors with free valuable information on computers and their accessories.

Some possible topics may include: Marketing, Computers and technology, Economics, Politics, Sports, Education, Creativity, Writing, Music, History, Tourism, Teach/learn a new language(s), Entertainment, Health, Lifestyle, Fashion and beauty, Gardening, Parenthood, Photography, Poems, Travel etc.

## How to drive visitors to the website or blog

- Use of relevant keywords on web pages (page properties on Frontpage) helps visitors find the website through search engines. Go to http://adwords.google.com and click on "Get Keyword ideas".

- Exchange links with other website owners by asking them to include on their website a link to your website while you do the same on yours.

- Share your web address with friends, relatives, coworkers and other people you know.

- Include signature (with your web address) on emails and other correspondences.

- Print out and distribute business cards, postcards with your web address.

- Find topics that the visitors would be interested in, publish it on the website and have the website updated on a regular basis

- Write articles on topics of interest and post on article directories such as www.Helium.com, www.ezinearticles.com and others with links back to your website or blog.

- Advertise through Google Adwords, Microsoft Adcenter and others with PPC (Pay-per-click). Most hosting plans provide credits for Adwords or Adcenter that can be used by first time customers. Pay-per-click advertising may turnout to be expensive because of competition and especially if the clicks do not bring enough revenue to the purchaser.

## How to keep in touch with website visitors

- Use newsletters to inform your visitors of newly published material and maintain communication

- Surveys and votes may be used to obtain feedback from visitors and help improve the website

- Blogs and podcasts are an excellent way to keep in touch with visitors because of the ability to leave comments

- Guestbook – with this however constant monitoring may be needed because it can also be used by spammers

- Publish something new regularly and request feedback

***Tip:*** Starting a business can be a challenge, however having determination, the right resources and competitive skills can be a great addition for any entrepreneur.

# STEP 10: Teaching children about money

| In summary, this chapter will cover: |
| --- |
| - Allowing children to earn money |
| - Letting children manage money |
| - Encouraging children to give to others |

The final step is to continuously learn about personal finance. There are a lot of changes taking place worldwide and it is helpful to keep on top of things by staying informed.

Join a library to read magazines, newspapers and borrow books about personal finance. Using the general knowledge acquired from various materials will provide guidance and facilitate the use of this information to make educated decisions about financial plans.

The Internet is a good source of information if the information can be verified by visiting multiple sources. Keywords that can be used while searching the Internet may include: Personal finance, money management, financial planning, investing in stocks and investing in bonds.

Using the information obtained from books, magazines, TV and radio parents can start teaching children while they are still young so that they can grow up to be financially responsible adults.

Parents are the best people to teach children about money. It is important to start teaching children by getting them involved in money management issues.

# Ways to help children develop money management skills

1. **Open a bank account.** Open a bank account in their name and put a specified amount on a monthly basis then encourage them to save. I remember my parents giving me a Postal Bank savings passbook on my 13th birthday and a National Bank of Commerce savings passbook when I turned 18. It was a tradition that they established for my siblings and I to help us understand the concept of saving and start practicing it. In addition parents can offer to match their children's savings efforts by contributing to their savings account exactly the same amount that children have decided to save from their pocket money. Owning a bank account will help children learn how to develop an organized way of saving and investing and will serve as a starting point for them to learn about the concept of interest rate.


2. **Open an "at-home-account".** A piggy bank at home is another simple way to teach children how to save. This could be anything from a homemade piggy bank such as a jar with a tight lid or a ready-made piggy bank that can be bought from kids' stores. A piggy bank provides a convenient and easy way to save. Money accumulated in the piggy bank can later be moved to the bank account.


3. **Develop financial goals.** Help the children develop financial goals, mainly short term and assist them in establishing strategies on how to accomplish their goals. Give them a piece of paper or better yet a note book which they can keep for years and encourage them to think of goals, put them in writing and discuss with you how they plan to accomplish them. This will provide them with a simple knowledge of personal financial planning techniques. They can review these goals every year to check the status and to adjust the goals or add new ones where necessary.

4. **Teach them "how to fish".** As the saying goes, give a man a fish and you have fed him for a day but teach him how to fish and you have fed him for a lifetime. The same goes for kids, get them to read simple money management books and magazines geared towards teaching children the principles of money and discuss what they think. These books and magazines can be found in libraries or online and you can print out results to keep for the future. Making it a routine to read these books and magazines will not only help them develop an interest in reading but also allow them to learn something new about money that they can put into practice.

5. **Let them earn some money.** Create jobs for the children to do for which they can be paid. At home children can be encouraged to do tasks in addition to the regular house chores (regular house chores should not be paid for) such as fixing the car or the house, redesigning the garden etc. for a small allowance. Also parents who bring home their work can give their children tasks that they can assist with. For example while growing up my mother who was a librarian at the time, would hire me part-time to help her arrange library catalog cards in alphabetical order. My dad extended me my first business loan to finance additional equipment after I managed to turn my hobby into a business. Unfortunately, three years and three employees later, I had to close the business so I could go to school full-time. A teacher can let their child help with filling out students' grades on a draft paper or computer, or typing draft exam questions on computer; a researcher can let them help with inputting data. Enlisting their help (based on their age) in return for a small payment will give them a chance (at a young age) to learn how to work hard, earn income, budget it, save and spend wisely. Parents can encourage entrepreneurial interests and support them whenever possible.

6. **Create a simple budget.** Children can be taught how to create and maintain a simple budget (monthly or semi-monthly depending on the frequency of their expenditures) for their school needs and other regular

needs. They can make a template, which they may reuse in the future. This will help them learn how to manage their expenditures to ensure that they do not spend beyond their means, which is the first rule of thumb of financial planning.

7. **Include them in regular financial tasks.** Allow children to participate in preparing or updating your budgets or when you are arranging to pay the bills. Invite them to be there when you are handling financial matters and take them through the process of what you are doing and why. This will give them a guideline, which they can use in the future.

8. **Allow them shop around.** With your help and depending on their age children can shop around (window shopping) for the best prices for items they need to buy such as school supplies (before they buy them) and be able to record prices and places so that next time they would have an idea of how much to budget for. This will help them develop practical ways to minimize their expenditures.

9. **Give them the freedom to shop.** Instead of buying items for children, allow them the freedom to plan for their own shopping by giving them the funds. Let them lead the way to where they would like to shop and what they would like to buy and later this experience can be used as an opportunity to first give praise for the hard work and then to point out any issues that may need attention as far as their shopping attitude. This will show that you believe in them and it will help build confidence in their abilities to manage their finances.

10. **Encourage a giving spirit.** Teach children how to give, first within the family and then to others outside the family. Encourage them to think of others and to donate something (they can start by giving just a little) for the

benefit of others. This teaches children that giving is about others and it can be more rewarding than receiving.

***Tip:*** Trusting children with money and showing them how to earn rather than to just receive money will enable them become better money managers in the future.

# Conclusion

Financial Planning is a continuous process. The main benefit of financial planning is the ability to plan for your money and allocate it where it is needed based on financial goals. Financial planning enables you to develop and monitor simple strategies that can be used to achieve financial independence and therefore take control of your money.

It is my hope that this book will be a personal guide to young professionals as they set out to build their careers, manage their hard earned money while at the same time giving to others in need.

In the next pages there are useful resources that can provide more information on the steps discussed in this book.

# Resources

Links that have been provided in this book are valid and working at the time the book is published. All links are provided for convenience only and do not reflect endorsement by the author.

## Websites

**Tanzania Financials Online** – online resource center for information on financial planning, investment, business and other related topics

http://www.tanzaniafinancials.com

**Bells Business Solutions** – (Provider of affordable web services, specifically Website Design/Creation, Online Marketing and Search Engine Optimization)
http://www.bellsbusiness.com

**Neptune Web Services** – Provider of reliable and low-cost domain name and web hosting services for individuals and small business entrepreneurs including those who have never created a website before.

http://www.neptunewebservices.com

**Financial Dictionary** – for definitions of financial terms
http://www.investopedia.com/dictionary/default.asp

**Dar es Salaam Stock Exchange** – Where publicly listed company shares/stocks and bonds are traded

http://www.dse.co.tz

**Nairobi Stock Exchange** – Where publicly listed company shares/stocks and bonds are traded

http://www.nse.co.ke


**Uganda Securities Exchange** – Where publicly listed company shares/stocks and bonds are traded

http://www.use.or.ug


**Central Bank of Tanzania** – http://www.bot-tz.org

**Central Bank of Kenya** – http://www.centralbank.go.ke

**Central Bank of Uganda** – http://www.bou.or.iug


**National Social Security Fund (NSSF)** – Provider of social security benefits at retirement and other benefits

http://www.nssftz.org


**Parastatal Pension Fund (PPF)** – Provider of pension benefits at retirement and other benefits

http://www.ppftz.org


**National Insurance Company (NIC)** – provider of insurance coverage
http://www.nictanzania.com


**Umoja Fund** – A Collective Investment Scheme that gives an opportunity for the majority of Tanzanian citizens to invest, take a stake in privatization, further participate in the capital markets and obtain a return on their investment.
http://www.utt-tz.org

**National Investment Company** - NICO is Collective Investment Scheme that combines stocks of several Tanzanian companies into one stock to be traded at the Dar es Salaam Stock Exchange.
http://www.nico.co.tz

**National Bureau of Statistics (Tanzania)** – Get the current inflation rate and information on other vital economic statistics.
http://www.nbs.go.tz

**Tanzania Investment Center (TIC)** – Provides information on investment opportunities in Tanzania, business establishment guidelines, licenses and other related information.
http://www.tic.co.tz

**Google Adsense** (earn income when visitors click on advertisements) –
https://www.google.com/adsense/login/en_US/?gsessionid=BZ09rH815F4

**Google Adwords** (Set up an advertising campaign to increase traffic and raise website revenue) – http://adwords.google.com/select/Login

**Free Articles Submission** (Submit articles for link exchange) –
http://www.freearticlesubmission.com/

**ScrubTheWeb** (free search engine optimization) -
http://www.scrubtheweb.com

**PRWeb** (submit press releases to market your online business) –
http://www.prweb.com/destination.php?awsrc=prwebsearch_fp&utm_sour
ce=YSM&utm_medium=PPC

**Lulu** (Self publish your books etc) – www.lulu.com

**Authorsden** (A community of Authors and Readers) – www.authorsden.com

**Helium** (where authors publish their works online) – www.helium.com

**PayPal** (accept payments online) - https://www.paypal.com/

**Quick Shopping Cart** (sell products and services online) - https://www.securepaynet.net/gdshop/ecommerce/cart.asp?prog_id=neptu newebservices&ci=1802&

# Banks

### CRDB Bank

http://www.crdbbank.com

### Tanzania Postal Bank

http://www.postalbank.co.tz

### National Bank of Commerce

http://www.nbctz.com

### National Microfinance Bank

http://www.nmbtz.com

### Stanbic Bank

http://www.stanbicbank.co.tz

### Standard Chartered Bank

http://www.standardchartered.com/tz

### Barclays Bank

http://www.barclays.com/africa/tanzania/index.html

### Exim Bank

http://www.eximbank-tz.com/

**FBME Bank**

http://www.fbme.com


**African Banking Corporation**

http://www.africanbankingcorp.com


**United Bank of Africa**

http://www.ubagroup.com


**Azania Bank**

http://www.azaniabank.co.tz


**Akiba Bancorp**

http://www.acb-bank.com

# Universities

University of Dar es Salaam

Hubert Kairuki Memorial University

Muhimbili University College of Health Science

The African Virtual University (AVU)

International Medical and technological University

Sokoine University of Agriculture

College of African Wildlife Management (MWEKA)

National Social Welfare Training Institute

# About the author

Juanita is an accountant and has worked at both for-profit and not-for-profit organizations. She previously worked at Pride headquarters as a Finance Officer. Before joining Pride, she worked part-time at the department of Economics of the University of Dar es Salaam, assisting with collection and processing of data for various economic research projects.

She has an MBA (Master of Business Administration) from Strayer Univesity in Maryland, United States and a Bachelors degree in Economics and Accounting from the University of Dar es Salaam, Tanzania. She is currently working on her Certificate of Financial Planning.

Juanita has written several articles for finance magazines including Tanzania Financials Online. Tanzania Financials Online is a resource center established in 2005 to provide financial, investment and business information for young professionals.

In her spare time, she likes to write and narrate children's stories and poems. However she enjoys the most, time spent with her husband Aloyce and two children Kennedy and Rachelle.

Juanita's memorable experiences include the growing up years spent with her siblings, Doris, Daudi and Amani, relatives and all the fun they had together.

To contact the author directly with comments or questions, send an email to jpkilasara@tanzaniafinancials.com

For more articles on personal finance visit www.tanzaniafinancials.com

www.ingramcontent.com/pod-product-compliance
Lightning Source LLC
Chambersburg PA
CBHW060626210326
41520CB00010B/1488